LITTORAL COMBAT SHIPS

BY PHILIP GREEN

Are you ready to take it to the extreme?
Torque books thrust you into the action-packed
world of sports, vehicles, and adventure. These books
may include dirt, smoke, fire, and dangerous stunts.
WARNING: read at your own risk.

Library of Congress Cataloging-in-Publication Data

Green, Philip, 1968-
  Littoral combat ships / by Philip Green.
      p. cm. – (Torque: military machines)
  Includes bibliographical references and index.
  Summary: "Amazing photography accompanies engaging information about Littoral Combat Ships.
The combination of high-interest subject matter and light text is intended for students in grades 3
through 7"–Provided by publisher.
  ISBN 978-1-60014-580-3 (hardcover : alk. paper)
  1. Littoral combat ships–Juvenile literature. I. Title.
  V883.A58 2011
  623.825'8–dc22   2010034497

This edition first published in 2011 by Bellwether Media, Inc.

The photographs in this book are reproduced through the courtesy of the United States Department
of Defense.

Printed in the United States of America, North Mankato, MN.
010111   1176

CONTENTS

THE LITTORAL COMBAT SHIP IN ACTION

The water is calm off the coast of an enemy country. A United States Navy fleet lies off the coast. The enemy is trying to move troops and weapons out to sea. A Littoral Combat Ship (LCS) moves in and uses its **sensors** to scan for enemy **mines**.

5

Two enemy ships open fire on the LCS. The LCS crew fires powerful guns at one of the ships. The enemy ship bursts into flames and begins to sink.

An MH-60R Seahawk helicopter takes off from the LCS. It flies toward the other enemy ship and fires a missile. The missile hits its target, and the ship explodes. The Seahawk returns to the LCS. The LCS must continue to patrol the enemy coast to keep the rest of the fleet safe.

SHALLOW-WATER DEFENSE

Littoral Combat Ships are the U.S. Navy's first line of defense in shallow waters. These coastal areas are called **littoral zones**. Littoral Combat Ships are fast and highly **maneuverable**. They can patrol in waters that larger warships cannot enter.

★ **FAST FACT** ★

The U.S. Navy plans to have a total of 55 Littoral Combat Ships before 2019.

USS Freedom

In 2004, the U.S. Navy asked for Littoral Combat Ships from two builders. Lockheed Martin built the LCS 1, which is also called the USS *Freedom*. It entered Navy service in 2008. General Dynamics built the LCS 2. It entered service in 2010 as the USS *Independence*. Both designs can perform the same missions.

USS Independence

WEAPONS AND FEATURES

The most important feature of an LCS is its ability to enter shallow waters. It needs a **hull** with a very shallow **draft** to do this. Both the *Independence* and *Freedom* have drafts of about 13 feet (4 meters).

Mk-110 57mm gun

Littoral Combat Ships use a variety of weapons to destroy enemy ships. An Mk-110 57mm gun can fire rounds at targets up to 9 miles (14.5 kilometers) away. Each LCS has at least two .50-caliber **machine guns**. They can also carry a RIM-116 Rolling Airframe Missile (RAM) launcher to shoot down enemy aircraft.

.50-caliber machine gun

RIM-116 Rolling Airframe Missile (RAM) launcher

An LCS can carry helicopters that help it attack enemy targets. The MH-60R Seahawk and the unmanned MQ-8 Fire Scout wait on deck until they are needed. These helicopters are armed with guns and missiles.

MH-60R Seahawk

MQ-8 Fire Scout

USS FREEDOM
SPECIFICATIONS:

Primary Function: Shallow-water defense

Length: 378 feet (115.2 meters)

Beam (width): 57.4 feet (17.5 meters)

Draft: 12.8 feet (3.9 meters)

Top Speed: 54 miles (87 kilometers) per hour

Range: 4,000 miles (6,437 kilometers)

Crew: up to 125

USS INDEPENDENCE
SPECIFICATIONS:

Primary Function: Shallow-water defense

Length: 418 feet (127.4 meters)

Beam (width): 104 feet (31.7 meters)

Draft: 13 feet (4 meters)

Top Speed: 51 miles (82 kilometers) per hour

Range: 4,950 miles (7,966 kilometers)

Crew: up to 75

LCS MISSIONS

Littoral Combat Ships can deal with a wide range of threats. The Navy outfits them with a special **mission package** for each type of mission. The mine warfare (MIW) package includes **sonar** and other sensors to detect enemy mines. An LCS can search for and destroy **submarines** with the anti-submarine warfare (ASW) package. The surface warfare (SUW) package has extra weapons for fighting enemy ships.

19

An LCS crew is split into groups. The core crew stays with the ship at all times. A **mission crew** joins an LCS for a specific mission. Each mission crew is trained to operate one of the LCS mission packages. An **aviation detachment** may be added to operate a ship's aircraft. The maximum number of crew members can be anywhere from 75 to 125. All crew members play an important role in making Littoral Combat Ships the future of coastal warfare.

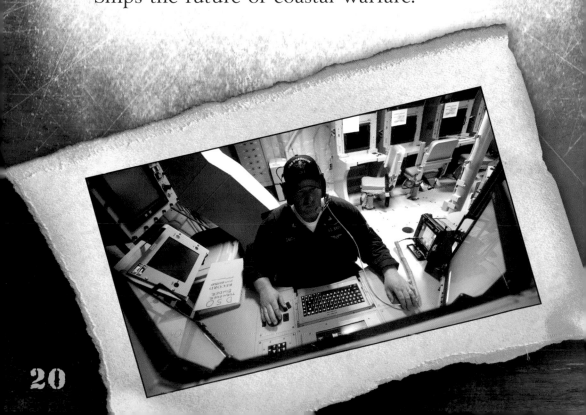

GLOSSARY

aviation detachment—crew members who can be added to an LCS to fly aircraft

draft—the depth the hull of a ship reaches in the water

hull—the body of a ship

littoral zones—areas of shallow water near coasts

machine guns—automatic weapons that rapidly fire bullets

maneuverable—able to move and change direction easily

mines—explosives that are set off when a person, vehicle, or ship touches or gets near them

mission crew—the crew that joins an LCS to operate the equipment in a mission package

mission package—a set of equipment added to an LCS for a specific mission

sensors—devices that give information about the terrain and the location of objects in the air and water

sonar—a sensor system that uses sound waves to locate objects underwater

submarines—warships that are able to travel underwater

TO LEARN MORE

AT THE LIBRARY

David, Jack. *United States Navy.* Minneapolis, Minn.: Bellwether Media, 2008.

Doeden, Matt. *The U.S. Navy.* Mankato, Minn.: Capstone Press, 2005.

Mueller, Richard. *Naval Warfare of the Future.* New York, N.Y.: Rosen Pub. Group, 2006.

ON THE WEB

Learning more about military machines is as easy as 1, 2, 3.

1. Go to www.factsurfer.com.

2. Enter "military machines" into the search box.

3. Click the "Surf" button and you will see a list of related Web sites.

With factsurfer.com, finding more information is just a click away.

INDEX